WHATEVER
IT TAKES

A JOURNEY INTO THE HEART
OF HUMAN ACHIEVEMENT

Thoughts to Inspire and Celebrate Your Commitment to Excellence™

By Bob Moawad with Dan Zadra

Designed by
Kobi Yamada and Steve Potter

COMPENDIUM™
INCORPORATED

live inspired.

ACKNOWLEDGEMENTS

The quotations in this book were gathered lovingly but unscientifically over several years and/or contributed by many friends and clients. Some arrived—and survived in our files—on scraps of paper and may therefore be imperfectly worded or attributed. Those that are attributed as "Keynotes" were drawn from the EDGE Keynote cards, 30 million of which have already been circulated throughout the world. To the authors, contributors and original sources, our thanks, and where appropriate, our apologies. —The Editors

ABOUT EDGE LEARNING INSTITUTE

For information on the worldwide programs conducted by Bob Moawad and the EDGE Learning Institute, call toll free 800-858-1484 or 800-682-2603.

WITH SPECIAL THANKS TO

Dick Anderson, Bill Cole, Maren Ellingson, Nancy Geier, Dennis Goin, Andrew Bennett, Skip Wilkins, Pat Gaddis, Sandy Jameson, Debbie Zak, Andrea Moawad, Bob Moawad, Jr., Trevor Moawad, and the rest of the team at EDGE Learning Institute.

CREDITS

Edited by Dan Zadra and Katie Lambert
Designed by Kobi Yamada and Steve Potter

A CALL TO **EXCELLENCE**

A GIFT TO INSPIRE
AND CELEBRATE YOUR
COMMITMENT TO EXCELLENCE

Long before the sun has risen or the people who deliver your morning newspaper have completed their rounds, millions of people are already wide-awake. Perhaps like you, they are restlessly and relentlessly pursuing their dreams.

Some are corporate executives, well-known celebrities, athletes, coaches, officials or leaders. But most are our neighbors, friends, relatives, employees or co-workers: The carpenter checking his tools; the sales manager packing her bags; the small business owner running spreadsheets on the kitchen computer; the teacher creating banners for the school assembly; the student athlete doing push-ups by his bed. The light is on in their windows, minds and hearts.

These are first-rate people in action—excellence, plain and simple. By doing whatever it takes to become the best they are capable of becoming, they lift our spirits. They stretch our boundaries. They energize our communities. And they bring new meaning to the terms, "job well-done" and "life well-led." Because you share that spirit, this book is dedicated to you.

Positively,

Bob Moawad

THE GIFT

The best day of your life is the one
on which you decide your life is
your own. No apologies or excuses.
No one to lean on, rely on, or
blame. The gift of life is yours—
it is an amazing journey—and
you alone are responsible for the
quality of it. This is the day your
life really begins.

Something wonderful, something hidden. A gift unique to you. Find it.

—UNKNOWN

For a while I looked outside to see what I could make the world give me, instead of looking inside to see what was there.

—BELL LIVINGSTONE

People talk about "finding" their lives. In reality, your life is not something you find—it's something you create.

—DAVID PHILLIPS

7

The greatest thing is, at any moment,
to be willing to give up who we are in
order to become all that we can be.

—MAX DEPREE

I was restless. I was doing okay,
but I was restless. One day it dawned
on me that I had been looking at life
through the wrong end of the telescope.
It was up to me to turn it around—
to make it bigger, better, more satisfying.

—ARNOLD SCHWARZENEGGER

Nothing is the worst
thing that can happen to us!

—RICHARD BACH

8

You don't need
to be sick to get better.

—DICK ANDERSON

Freedom is nothing else
but a chance to be better.

—ALBERT CAMUS

9

It's your life,
your one and only life—
so take excellence
very personally.

—SCOTT JOHNSON

Champions are born…
and then unmade.

–CONVERSE AD

Don't be afraid to give up
the good to go for the great.

–JOHN D. ROCKEFELLER

You only live once—but if you work
it right, once is enough.

–JOE E. LEWIS

10

"Is life worth living?"
The question does not make any sense.

—ERICH FROMM

In the Auschwitz death camp, a
group of inmates told Viktor Frankl that
they no longer expected anything from
life. Frankl responded that they had it
backward. "Life expects something of
you, and it is up to every individual to
discover what it should be."

—UNKNOWN

Life is ours to be spent,
not saved.

—D.H. LAWRENCE

Begin doing what you
want to do now. We are not living in
eternity. We have only this moment,
sparkling like a star in our hand—
and melting like a snowflake.

—MARIE BEYON RAY

12

One of these days is none of these days.

—ENGLISH PROVERB

No, you never get any fun
out of things you haven't done.

—OGDEN NASH

Neglect not the gift that is in thee.

–NEW TESTAMENT

I wouldn't miss life for anything!

–UNKNOWN

Alas for those who never sing but die
with all their music still in them.

–OLIVER WENDELL HOLMES

THE GIFT

> IT'S NOT WHO WE ARE
> THAT HOLDS US BACK,
> IT'S WHO WE THINK
> WE'RE NOT.
> –Michael Nolan

THE FREEDOM

Allow yourself the freedom to grow and expand. Form the habit of saying yes to your own potential. Take time to think of all the reasons why you can and why you will excel at something wonderful…because there will always be plenty of people around to tell you why you can't.

Discover your possibilities.

—DR. ROBERT SCHULLER

The greatest crime in the world
is not developing your potential.
When you do what you do best,
you are helping not only
yourself, but the world.

—ROGER WILLIAMS

15

You don't get to choose how you're
going to die. Or when. You can only
decide how you're going to live. Now.

—JOAN BAEZ

If we did all the things
we are capable of, we would
literally astound ourselves.

–THOMAS EDISON

Help! I'm being held "prisoner"
by my heredity and environment.

–DENNIS ALLEN

It's not trespassing when you
cross your own boundaries.

–JOHNNIE WALKER

Caution! The left-brained
world wants you to be "realistic," and
"quit dreaming," and "get your head out
of the clouds," and "get your feet on the
ground," and "be just like us."
To advance and prosper,
steadfastly ignore that advice.

–MARILYN GREY

17

There has never been another you.
With no effort on your part you were
born to be something very special and
set apart. What you are going to do
in appreciation of that gift is a
decision only you can make.

–DAN ZADRA

They say you can't do it, but
sometimes it doesn't always work.

–CASEY STENGEL

If you're strong enough,
there are no precedents.

–F. SCOTT FITZGERALD

18

Be faithful to that which
exists nowhere but in yourself.

–ANDRÉ GIDE

Anytime you poke your head
above the crowd, someone will
take a poke at it.

–UNITED TECHNOLOGIES

Just remember that you don't
have to be what they want you to be.

–MUHAMMAD ALI

19

To be nobody but yourself
in a world which is doing its best,
day and night, to make you like everybody else is to fight the hardest battle
which any human being can fight...
but never stop fighting!

–E.E. CUMMINGS

If you truly expect to realize your dreams, abandon the need for blanket approval. If conforming to everyone else's expectations is the number one goal, you have sacrificed your uniqueness and, therefore, your excellence.

—DON WARD

20

Most of our limitations are self-imposed. Roger Bannister was the first human to run a sub-four-minute mile—a barrier that was previously deemed insurmountable. Immediately after Bannister proved it was "possible," runners all over the world repeated his feat.

—BOB MOAWAD

Never tell a young person that
something cannot be done. God may
have waited centuries for someone
ignorant enough of the impossible
to do that very thing.

—J.R. HOLMES

Records are set all the time by big-
hearted people who don't have the right
background, ability or experience—or
who simply don't know any better.

—KOBI YAMADA

Remember always that you not only
have the right to be an individual,
you have an obligation to be one.

—ELEANOR ROOSEVELT

21

IMAGINATION IS
EVERYTHING. IT
IS THE PREVIEW
OF LIFE'S COMING
ATTRACTIONS.
–Albert Einstein

THE DREAM

Dreams are the picture-making power of your imagination. They are the stuff of which life, hope, love, fun, accomplishment and excellence are made. All great things are born there. Respect and nurture your dreams—believe in them—and bring them to the sunshine and the light.

Keep true to the
dreams of thy youth.

–FRIEDRICH VON SCHILLER

At least once a day,
allow yourself the freedom to
think and dream for yourself.

–ALBERT EINSTEIN

Most of us are so busy doing
what we think we have to do,
that we do not think about
what we really want to do.

–UNKNOWN

THE DREAM

"Why not?" is a slogan
for an interesting life.

–MASON COOLEY

You have to think anyway,
so why not think big?

–DONALD TRUMP

24

We can only thrive when we have
a goal—a passionate purpose which
bears upon the public interest.

–MARGARET E. KUHN

High expectations
are the key to everything.

—SAM WALTON

Most people don't aim too high
and miss, they aim too low and hit.

—BOB MOAWAD

Is not life a hundred times
too short for us to bore ourselves?

—FRIEDRICH NIETZSCHE

THE DREAM

Your dreams are not meant
to put you to sleep, but to alert
and arouse you to your
immense possibilities.

—DAVID PHILLIPS

You're damn right it's possible.
If you dreamed it up, it's possible.
You're the only person who can say,
"It's impossible."

—CARLO MENTA

Extraordinary people visualize
not what is possible or probable, but
rather what is impossible. And by
visualizing the impossible, they
begin to see it as possible.

—CHERIE CARTER-SCOTT

THE DREAM

Those who dream by night wake
to find that it was vanity. But the
dreamers of day are dangerous;
they may act out their dreams with
open eyes to make it possible.

–T. E. LAWRENCE

27

Always dream and shoot
higher than you know you can do.
Don't bother just to be better than
your contemporaries or predecessors.
Try to be better than yourself.

–WILLIAM FAULKNER

THE DREAM

The prize goes to the person
who sees the future the quickest.

–WILLIAM STIRITZ

There are two worlds: The world
that we can measure with line and rule,
and the world we feel with our hearts
and imaginations.

–LEIGH HUNT

The man who has
no imagination has no wings.

–MUHAMMAD ALI

28

Dreams are what get you started.
Discipline is what keeps you going.

—JIM RYUN

We must teach our children
to dream with their eyes open.

—HARRY EDWARDS

29

Forever be a dreamer!
When your memories outnumber
your dreams, the end is near.

—EDGE KEYNOTE

THE DREAM

A GOAL IS A DREAM
WITH ITS FEET ON
THE GROUND.
—Frank Vizzare

THE GOAL

You don't have to take life
the way it comes to you.
By converting your dreams
into goals, and your goals
into plans, you can design
your life to come to you the
way you want it. You can
live your life on purpose,
instead of by chance.

A dream without a goal
is just a wish.

—BILL COLE

It takes as much energy to wish
as it does to plan.

—ELEANOR ROOSEVELT

Concentrate on finding your goal,
then concentrate on reaching it.

—MICHAEL FRIEDSAM

If you don't know where you're going,
you might wind up someplace else.

–CASEY STENGEL

People are like guided missiles.
Without a target, they wander
aimlessly across the horizon and
eventually self-destruct.

–EDGE KEYNOTE

There is only one success—to be able to
spend your life in your own way.

–CHRISTOPHER MORLEY

32

The best way to predict
the future is to invent it.

—ALAN KAY

The world is before you,
and you need not take it or leave
it as it was when you came in.

—JAMES BALDWIN

Planning is bringing the future
into the present so that you can
do something about it now.

—ALAN LAKEIN

The world stands aside to let anyone pass who knows where he is going.

—DAVID STARR JORDAN

What do you want to do?
What do you want to be? What do you want to have? Where do you want to go? Who do you want to go with? How the hell do you plan to get there? Write it down. Go do it. Enjoy it. Share it. It doesn't get much simpler or better than that.

—LEE IACOCCA

Love and do what you will.

—ST. AUGUSTINE

Progress comes from caring
more about what needs to be done
than about who gets the credit.

–DOROTHY HEIGHT

Goals give purpose.
Purpose gives faith. Faith gives
courage. Courage gives enthusiasm.
Enthusiasm gives energy. Energy gives
life. Life lifts you over the bar.

–BOB RICHARDS, POLE VAULTER

When we set exciting worthwhile goals for ourselves, they work
in two ways: We work on them,
and they work on us.

–BOB MOAWAD

35

THE GOAL

Dreams whet your appetite,
but goals make you hungry.

–JOSIE BISSETT

We all love big ideas.
If an organization lacks enthusiasm,
if the people are bored, it's time for a
big idea. The moment you set a new
goal, you create a gap between where
you are and where you really
want to be. The urge to close that
gap generates tension, energy,
enthusiasm, purpose and drive.

–HARRY GRAY

36

Set exciting personal goals.
You will live longer.

—BOB MOAWAD

Keep changing,
because when you're through
changing—you're through.

—BERT-OLAF SVANHOLM

Two roads diverged
in a wood, and I—
I took the one less traveled by,
And that has made
all the difference.

—ROBERT FROST

THE GOAL

THE PLUNGE

Indecision and second-guessing are the mortal enemies of spontaneous brilliance and planning. Without action, your dream, goal or plan has little meaning in the world. Living and risking are close companions. If you sense that you have made a good decision, have faith. Move forward.

A life not put to the test
is not worth living.

–EPICTECUS

Courage is the capacity to
confront what can be imagined.

–LEO ROSTEN

39

You must get involved
to have an impact. No one
is impressed with the
won/lost record of the referee.

–NAPOLEON HILL

There's as much risk in doing
nothing as in doing something.

–TRAMMELL CROW

Action without planning is fatal,
but planning without action is futile.

–UNKNOWN

40

If you put everything off till you're
sure of it, you'll get nothing done.

–NORMAN VINCENT PEALE

You cannot lead
where you do not go.

–MARY KAY ASH

If you don't execute your ideas…
they'll die.

–ROBERT PERCIVAL

A year from now you will wish
you had started today.

–KAREN LAMB

If you have a dream,
give it a chance to happen.

–RICHARD DEVOS

Often you have to
rely on your intuition.

–BILL GATES

42

We wouldn't worry nearly as much
about what others thought of us, if
we recognized how seldom they did.

–EDGE KEYNOTE

If you're going to worry, don't do it.
If you do it, don't worry.

—MICHAEL NOLAN

Action may not always
bring happiness, but there is
no happiness without action.

—BENJAMIN DISRAELI

43

The moment you commit and quit
holding back, all sorts of unforeseen
incidents, meetings and material
assistance will rise up to help you.
The simple act of commitment is
a powerful magnet for help.

—NAPOLEON HILL

There comes a moment when
you have to stop revving up the car
and shove it into gear.

–DAVID MAHONEY

44

You miss 100 percent
of the shots you never take.

–WAYNE GRETZKY, PRO HOCKEY PLAYER

Just do it.

–NIKE AD

I'd rather be sorry for something
I did than for something I didn't do.

—RAY PRICE

Be not the slave of your own past—
plunge into the sublime seas, dive deep,
and swim far, so you shall come back
with self-respect, with new power, with
an advanced experience that shall
explain and overlook the old.

—RALPH WALDO EMERSON

For of all sad words of tongue
or pen, the saddest are these:
"It might have been."

—JOHN GREENLEAF WHITTIER

THE
MISTAKES

Fail forward! Whenever you undertake a new project, attempt to make as many mistakes as rapidly as possible in order to learn as much as you can in the shortest period of time. Mistakes are great. Learn from them; research them; use them to propel you forward.

If at first you don't succeed,
you're in great company.

—ELDEN PETERSON

Jockey Eddie Arcaro lost his first
45 races. Michael Jordan was cut
from his high school basketball team.
You will not be remembered for the
number of times you failed in the
beginning, but for the number of
times you succeeded in the end.

—DAN ZADRA

If you get off to a bad start,
don't worry. It's the finish
not the start that counts.

—EDGE KEYNOTE

How do I work? I grope.

—ALBERT EINSTEIN

Results? Why, man,
I have gotten a lot of results.
I know several thousand things
that won't work.

—THOMAS EDISON

Those who never made a mistake
probably never made a discovery.

—SAMUEL SMILES

48

Error is only the opportunity
to begin again, more intelligently.

–HENRY FORD

Most of my advances were
by mistake. You uncover what is
when you get rid of what isn't.

–BUCKMINSTER FULLER

A mistake is simply another
way of doing things.

–KATHARINE GRAHAM

49

No more mistakes
and you're through.

—JOHN KLEISS

Demand perfection of
yourself and you'll seldom attain it.
Fear of making a mistake is the
biggest single cause of making one.
Relax—pursue excellence, not perfection.

—BUD WINTER, TRACK COACH

A mistake only proves that
someone stopped talking long
enough to do something.

—MICHAEL LEBOEUF

The fastest way to succeed
is to double your failure rate.

–THOMAS J. WATSON

Critics hang around and
wait for others to make mistakes.
But the real doers of the world
have no time for criticizing others.
They're too busy doing, making
mistakes, improving, making progress.

–DR. WAYNE DYER

51

Life is like playing the
violin solo in public and learning
the instrument as you go along.

–SAMUEL BUTLER

THE MISTAKES

For God's sake give me
someone who has brains enough
to make a fool of himself.

–ROBERT LOUIS STEVENSON

52

Quit sitting up there in the bleachers.
Come on down on the field. Suit up!
Roll around in the dirt! Take a chance
on missing a pass, fumbling the ball or
making a jackass out of yourself. That's
what the champions are willing to do.

–"MISTAKES ARE GREAT"

Mistakes are evidence that
you're human—and what's
wrong with being human?

–EDGE KEYNOTE

Mistakes are part of the
dues one pays for a full life.

–SOPHIA LOREN

If all else fails, immortality can always
be assured by spectacular error.

–JOHN KENNETH GALBRAITH

In the end, there are no mistakes.
There is only yearning and learning.

–DAN ZADRA

THE
PASSION

If you love what you do, and you
feel that it matters, then the
passion will show. In today's
world, "I care" is not just a nice
phrase—it's a two-word recipe
for excellence, success and
fulfillment. It all boils down
to those who really care and
those who really don't.

Don't care what others
think of what you do; but care
very much about what you
think you do.

—ST. FRANCIS DE SALES

Caring is a powerful
business advantage.

—SCOTT JOHNSON

Passion persuades.

—ANITA RODDICK, THE BODY SHOP

Nothing splendid was ever created
in cold blood. Heat is required to forge
anything. Every great accomplishment
is the story of a flaming heart.

—ARNOLD GLASOW

56

Intensity for immensity.

—RUSSELL JONES

Success is never the result
of spontaneous combustion.
You must set yourself on fire.

—ARNOLD GLASOW

I believe that a
person ought to know what
he believes, why he believes it,
and then believe it.

—CHARLES "TREMENDOUS" JONES

Fall in love with what you do;
believe in what you're doing;
strive to continuously improve.

—BOB MOAWAD

When you truly believe in
something, and you carry it
in your heart, you accept
no excuses, only results.

—KEN BLANCHARD

57

Dedication to excellence
on any level, in any area, requires
an intensity of emotional investment.
Unfortunately, there are scores of people
who do not make the investment—who
do not feel strongly about anything.

–THEODORE ISAAC RUBIN

Be fanatics. When it comes
to being, doing and dreaming
the best, be maniacs.

–A.M. ROSENTHAL

I realized a long time ago that a belief
which does not spring from a conviction
in the emotions is no belief at all.

–EVELYN SCOTT

THE PASSION

No matter how long I live there
will never be a dull moment.

–HARRIET DOERR

I never went to work,
I always went to play.

–WILLIE STARGELL, PRO BASEBALL PLAYER

There ain't no rules around here.
We're trying to accomplish something.

–THOMAS EDISON

59

Pressure is neither good nor bad.
You can convert pressure into negative
tension and worry—or positive
expectation and enthusiasm.
It's a choice you make yourself.

—EDGE KEYNOTE

If you feel happy, tell your face.

—STEVE POTTER

While designing Apple Computer's
new Macintosh, Steve Jobs flew a
pirate flag over his building to signify
his team's determination to blow all
rival teams out of the water.

—DAN ZADRA

60

There is only one big thing—desire.
And before it, when it is big, all is little.

—WILLA CATHER

If I had to nominate a driving force in
my life, I'd plump for passion every time.
My passionate belief is that business can
be fun, it can be conducted with love and
a powerful force for good.

—ANITA RODDICK, THE BODY SHOP

Go put your creed into your deed.

—RALPH WALDO EMERSON

THE PASSION

THE
COMMITMENT

Anybody can quit. It's exactly what your
adversaries or competitors hope you
will do, and there's always a legitimate
excuse. But have faith; hang in there.
Stay in touch with your dream and commitment. Remember that your resources
are always far deeper and far greater
than you ever imagine them to be. You
got yourself this far. Down deep you've
got what it takes to go the distance.

Folks, we're going on a journey.
On this journey we will carry our
wounded and shoot the dissenters.

–"REENGINEERING THE CORPORATION"

To finish first,
you must first finish.

–RICK MEARS

63

Commitment is the stuff character
is made of; the power to change the
face of things. It is the daily triumph
of integrity over skepticism.

–UNKNOWN

THE COMMITMENT

To be a champion
you have to believe in yourself
when no one else will.

—SUGAR RAY ROBINSON

Ignore people who say
it can't be done.

—ELAINE RIDEOUT

Others can stop you temporarily.
Only you can do it permanently.

—EDGE KEYNOTE

Only when I fall
do I get up again.

–VINCENT VAN GOGH

In times of difficulty, you may
feel that your problems will go on and
on, but they won't. Every mountain has
a top. Every problem has a life span.
The question is, who is going to give in
first, the frustration or you?

–DR. ROBERT SCHULLER

Problems come and go.
I'm in it for the long haul.

–GEORGE BURNS

The biggest enemy is doubt.
If you don't believe in what you are
doing, you aren't going to make it.

–PHILIPPE KAHN

I attribute my success to this:
I never gave or took any excuse.

–FLORENCE NIGHTINGALE

The great question is not
whether you have failed, but whether
you are content with failure.

–ABRAHAM LINCOLN

66

We are all faced with a series
of great opportunities brilliantly
disguised as unsolvable problems.

–JOHN W. GARDNER

Faith and doubt are both
needed—not as antagonists, but
working side by side—to take us
around the unknown curve.

–LILLIAN SMITH

What is defeat? Nothing but
education, nothing but the first
step toward something better.

–WENDELL PHILLIPS

THE COMMITMENT

Doubt whom you will,
but never yourself.

—CHRISTIAN NESTELL BOVEE

He who has a why to live for
can bear with almost any how.

—FRIEDRICH NIETZSCHE

Perhaps I am
stronger than I think.

—THOMAS MERTON

Show me someone who has done
something worthwhile, and I'll show you
someone who has overcome adversity.

–LOU HOLTZ

I am not concerned that you have fallen;
I am concerned that you arise.

–ABRAHAM LINCOLN

I encourage my students never
to give up on their dream, to emulate
effort above all, and to mix passion
with discipline so as to make the most
of luck when it strikes.

–DAVID PHILLIPS

THE ATTITUDE

Attitudes are habits of thought that predict or perpetuate our performance. We aren't born with them—they are acquired. Notice that the most interesting and successful people have acquired the habit of talking about what they are for rather than what they are against. Their optimism pulls and propels them forward. They lean into life rather than away from it. How about you? Do you see difficulties behind every opportunity, or opportunities behind every difficulty?

Everything can be taken from man
but one thing: the last of the human
freedoms—to choose one's attitude in
any given set of circumstances,
to choose one's own way.

–VIKTOR FRANKL

We cannot tell what may
happen to us in the strange medley
of life. But we can decide what
happens in us, how we take it,
what we do with it—and that is
what really counts in the end.

–JOSEPH FORT NEWTON

THE ATTITUDE

Pain is inevitable; suffering is optional.

—UNKNOWN

Your mind can focus on fear,
worry, problems, negativity or despair.
Or it can focus on confidence,
opportunity, solutions, optimism
and success. You decide.

—DON WARD

When one door closes another
door opens; but we often look so
longingly and so regretfully upon
the door that closed, that we fail to
see the one that has opened for us.

—HELEN KELLER

Losers always have an excuse;
Winners always have an idea.
Losers fix the blame;
Winners fix the situation.
Losers make promises;
Winners keep commitments.
Losers let it happen;
Winners make it happen.
Losers say, "Why don't they do
something?" Winners say,
"Here's something I can do."

—EDGE KEYNOTE

Attitudes are contagious.
Do you want people around
you to catch yours?

—BOB MOAWAD

THE ATTITUDE

Give your positive emotions a job.

–RALPH M. FORD

I realize that a sense of humor isn't for
everyone. It's only for people who want
to have fun, enjoy life, and feel alive.

–ANNE WILSON SCHAEF

Are you paying too much
attention to minor irritations?
Life is too short to be little.

–EDGE KEYNOTE

Don't lose your head.
It's the best part of your body.

—JIMMY SNYDER

If you're anticipating the worst
while hoping for the best, you will
usually get the worst. Turn it around!
Imagine the best, expect the best
and you'll usually get the best.

—DAN ZADRA

"I must do something"
will always solve more problems
than "Something must be done."

—BITS & PIECES

75

Some favorite expressions of small children: "It's not my fault... They made me do it...I forgot." Some favorite expressions of small adults: "It's not my job...No one told me... It couldn't be helped." True freedom begins and ends with personal accountability.

–DAN ZADRA

76

When building a team, always look for people who love to win. If you can't find any of those, search for people who hate to lose.

–ROSS PEROT

They can because
they think they can.

−VIRGIL

Be absolutely determined
to enjoy what you do.

−GERRY SIKORSKI

The happiest people seem to be those
who have no particular reason for being
happy except that they are.

−WILLIAM RALPH INGE

77

THE ATTITUDE

THE DRIVE

We all get 24 hours a day. It's the only fair thing; it's the only thing that's equal. It's up to us to determine what we do with those 24 hours. We can waste them, or we can choose to consistently fill them with good. Preparation, practice, hustle, grit, initiative and drive—these are all old-fashioned words, but they have built the world.

What is it going to be—
reasons or results?

–ART TUROCK

You can't make footprints
in the sands of time if you're sitting
on your butt. And who wants to make
buttprints in the sands of time?

–BOB MOAWAD

Spectacular achievement is always
preceded by unspectacular preparation.

–DR. ROBERT SCHULLER

79

If I just work when the spirit
moves me, the spirit will ignore me.

—CAROLYN FORCHÉ

Beethoven, Wagner, Bach and
Mozart all worked regular shifts each
day, just like an accountant settles in
at the computer. They did not sit down
to work because they were inspired,
but became inspired because they
sat down to work.

—UNKNOWN

I hated every minute of the training,
but I said, "Don't quit. Suffer now and
live the rest of your life as a champion."

—MUHAMMAD ALI

I see no virtue where I smell no sweat.

—FRANCIS QUARLES

To every person there comes that special moment when he is tapped on the shoulder to do a very special thing unique to him. What a tragedy if that moment finds him unprepared for the work that would be his finest hour.

—WINSTON CHURCHILL

81

We say we waste time, but that is impossible. We waste ourselves.

—ALICE BLOCH

Prepare! The time will come
when winter will ask what you
were doing all summer.

–HENRY CLAY

No one has ever drowned
in his own sweat.

–ANN LANDERS

One of life's most painful
moments comes when we must
admit that we didn't do our homework,
that we are not prepared.

–MERLIN OLSEN

When you're not practicing,
remember that someone somewhere
is practicing, and when you meet
him he will win.

—ED MACAULEY

Tears will get you sympathy.
Sweat will get you change.

—JESSE JACKSON

Life's most persistent and
urgent question is: What are
you doing for others?

—MARTIN LUTHER KING, JR.

The best way out
is always through.

–ROBERT FROST

The harder you work,
the harder it is to surrender.

–VINCE LOMBARDI

84

He who strives unceasingly,
him we can redeem, and should.

–JOHANN VON GOETHE

I've never lost a game in my life.
Once in a while, time ran out on me.

–BOBBY LAYNE, NFL QUARTERBACK

When you put a limit on what
you will do, you have put a limit on
what you can do.

–CHARLES SCHWAB

When you have done your best,
await the result in peace.

–EDGE KEYNOTE

THE
ESTEEM

From the time we are little children, we are reminded to "Love our neighbors as ourselves," and the interesting thing is, we always do! To determine the degree to which individuals like and respect themselves, simply watch the way they treat the people around them. Consideration, thoughtfulness, integrity, candor, character and class—these are all distinguishing characteristics of people with sound self-esteem, the people we love, respect, follow and admire.

People who matter are most
aware that everyone else does, too.

–MALCOLM FORBES

People with humility don't think
less of themselves—they just think
about themselves less.

–NORMAN VINCENT PEALE

87

Each day silently affirm
that you are the type of person with
whom you would like to spend
the rest of your life.

–BOB MOAWAD

Have unconditional warm
regards for all people at all times.
Treat everyone, including and especially
yourself, with consideration and respect.

—EDGE KEYNOTE

If you're too busy to help the people
around you succeed, you're too busy.

—BOB MOAWAD

If you insist on measuring yourself,
put the tape around your heart rather
than your head. Try measuring
your wealth by who you are,
rather than what you have.

—CAROL TRABELLE

THE ESTEEM

Whenever you are to do a thing,
though it can never be known but
to yourself, ask yourself how you would
act were all the world looking at you,
and act accordingly.

–THOMAS JEFFERSON

We must have good domestic
relations with ourselves before we can
have good foreign relations with others.

–JOSHUA LOTH LIEBMAN

89

Those you followed passionately, gladly
and zealously have made you feel like
somebody. It wasn't merely the job title
or power—they somehow made you
feel terrific to be around them.

–IRWIN FEDERMAN

If you don't place a high value
on your talents, who will? If you
don't think highly of yourself,
why would anyone?

—EDGE KEYNOTE

People are in greater need of your
praise when they try and fail, than
when they try and succeed.

—BOB MOAWAD

Accept compliments easily and share
your successes with others who have
contributed to them. No one ever goes
alone to the heights of excellence.

—EDGE KEYNOTE

90

Everyone appreciates being appreciated.
Catch people red-handed in the act
of doing something right each day—
and praise them for it.

–BOB MOAWAD

To be truly free and to grow
in self-esteem, choose not to give up
your growth, pursuit of fulfillment or
happiness to anyone. Choose to treat
yourself with dignity and proceed to
move toward full love, wisdom, freedom
and joy, knowing that you are the
authority over you.

–LILBURN BARKSDALE

THE ESTEEM

It's the greatest compliment to
be humble. You want to be the best
you can be, but not compare yourself
with others. I'd just like to be seen as
someone maximizing my own talents.

—HAKEEM OLAJUWON

Character is what you are in the dark.

—DWIGHT L. MOODY

Have the courage to say no.
Have the courage to face the truth.
Do the right thing because it is right.
These are the magic keys to living
your life with integrity.

—W. CLEMENT STONE

Love cures people—
both the ones who give it and
the ones who receive it.

–KARL MENNINGER

They are strong who can laugh
at themselves and cry for others.

–KOBI YAMADA

Know you're good, wear it well
and share it with others. Self-esteem
is the degree to which you like and
respect yourself and feel confident
in dealing with life's challenges.

–EDGE KEYNOTE

THE ESTEEM

THE EDGE

The difference between the bottom and the top, between success and failure, between mediocrity and excellence, is often very small. A single insight is sometimes worth a life's experience. The accumulation of a lot of little things isn't little. So breathe in experience. Remain a lifelong learner. Fine-tune your skills and sweat the details. Constantly be on the look-out for the little difference that can make a big difference.

Those who think they know it all
have no way of finding out they don't.

–LEO BUSCAGLIA

Education consists mainly
in what we have unlearned.

–MARK TWAIN

95

If at first you don't succeed,
before you try again, stop to figure
out what you did wrong.

–LEO ROSTEN

You can work at something
for twenty years and come away
with twenty years' worth of valuable
experience, or you can come away with
one year's experience twenty times.

–GWEN JACKSON

Neil Eskelin watched in wonder
as a tiny ant struggled to carry a large
piece of straw. Blocked by a deep crack
in the ground, the ant carefully laid
the piece of straw across the gap and
walked to the other side. What
appeared to be a burden for the
ant was actually his freedom!

–UNKNOWN

Beware of those who
won't be bothered with details.

–WILLIAM FEATHER

Don't just learn the tricks of the trade.
Learn the trade.

–JAMES BENNIS

Focus on your natural strengths
and abilities. Exploit what you have,
not what you don't have.

–ERIC OSSERMON

Most ball games are lost, not won.

—CASEY STENGEL

Winners have simply formed the habit
of doing things losers don't like to do.

—ALBERT GRAY

Everybody has to try just a
little bit harder, do just a little
bit better, think just a little deeper,
work just a little longer.

—MARY LOU RETTON

The fifty-goal scorer sees the back of the net; the five-goal scorer can tell you the brand name of the pads on every goalie in the league.

–WAYNE GRETZKY, PRO HOCKEY PLAYER

Inches make champions.

–VINCE LOMBARDI

There is greatness all around you— use it. It is easy to be great when you get around great people.

–BOB RICHARDS

It's not the amount of time
you devote, but what you devote
to the time that counts.

—EDGE KEYNOTE

Oh, the difference between
nearly right and exactly right.

—H. JACKSON BROWN

In order to succeed,
at times you have to make
something from nothing.

—RUTH MICKLEBY-LAND

100

In a time of drastic change, it is
the learners who will inherit the future.

—ERIC HOFFER

You will never "find" time for anything.
If you want time, you must make it.

—CHARLES BUXTON

When you have exhausted all
possibilities, remember this—
you haven't.

—EDGE KEYNOTE

THE STANDARDS

It's a competitive world out there, with each of us contributing something new and, hopefully, better to it. Every day, in every little corner of that world, someone somewhere is pushing the quality of their product, service or work—their standards—a little higher, a little closer to the heights of excellence. Set your own standards, but be inspired by the work of others. Continuously learn from it. Build on it. Challenge it. Surpass it!

Nobody knows what is
the best he can do.

—ARTURO TOSCANINI

Excellence is not a spectator sport.
Everyone's involved.

—JACK WELCH

103

First we will be best,
and then we will be first.

—GRANT TINKER

A competitive world offers
two possibilities. You can lose.
Or, if you want to win,
you can change.

—LESTER THUROW

Be grateful for competition.
When your competitors upset your
plans or outdo your designs, they
open the infinite possibilities of
your own work to you.

—GIL ATKINSON

Ruthlessly compete with your
own best self.

—APOLLO 13 ENGINEERS

Continuous improvement is
impossible without continuous
innovation.

–DON GALER

Almost means not quite.
Not quite means not right.
Not right means wrong. Wrong
means the opportunity to
start again and get it right.

–DAN ZADRA

Do it. Do it right. Do it right now.

–NASA SLOGAN

If you keep doing what
you've always done, you'll keep
getting what you've always got…
if you're fortunate.

–BOB MOAWAD

Someone once asked me if there
wasn't benefit in overlooking one
small flaw. "What is a small flaw?"
I asked him.

–DON SHULA

Hold yourself responsible for a higher
standard than anybody else expects of
you. Never excuse yourself.

–HENRY WARD BEECHER

Who wants to be average?
Average is that place in the middle.
It's the best of the worst, or the
worst of the best.

–BOB MOAWAD

I could use a hundred people
who don't know there is such a word
as impossible.

–HENRY FORD

Impossible only defines
the degree of difficulty.

–DAVID PHILLIPS

Those who stop
being better stop being good.

—OLIVER CROMWELL

People who are resting on
their laurels are wearing them
on the wrong end.

—MALCOLM KUSHNER

Never mistake goodwill
for the deed.

—FRANK VIZZARE

108

If what you did yesterday
seems big, you haven't done
anything today.

—LOU HOLTZ

Growth is the only evidence of life.

—CARDINAL NEWMAN

If you won't be better
tomorrow than you were today, then
what do you need tomorrow for?

—RABBI NACHMAN OF BRATSLAV

THOUGHTS
FOR THE
ROAD

Eleanor Roosevelt loved to say that the future belongs to those who believe in the beauty of their dreams. In the long run, we really do shape our own lives; and then together we shape the world around us. The process never ends until we die, and the choices we make are ultimately our responsibility. So choose wisely, boldly and confidently. Believe that your choices make a difference—they do!—and enjoy these final thoughts to accompany you on the journey. Here's to you— and to excellence in all that you do.

Remember that you are unique.
If that is not fulfilled, then something
wonderful has been lost.

—MARTHA GRAHAM

It is never too late to be what
you might have been.

—GEORGE ELIOT

Don't let anyone steal your dream.
It's your dream, not theirs.

—DAN ZADRA

Never compromise yourself.
You are all you've got.

—JANIS JOPLIN

There are only two things you
"have to" do in life. You "have to"
die and you "have to" live until you die.
You make up all the rest.

—MARILYN GREY

What people say you cannot do,
you try and find that you can.

—HENRY DAVID THOREAU

Never place a period
where God has placed a comma.

–GRACIE ALLEN

Realize that nothing is
too good to be true.

–KOBI YAMADA

Some things have to be believed
to be seen.

–RALPH HODGSON

113

No matter what the statistics say,
there's always a way.

—BERNIE SIEGEL, M.D.

Be assured that you'll always
have time for the things you put first.

—LIANE STEELE

I don't want to get to the
end of my life and find that I
lived the length of it. I want to have
lived the width of it as well.

—DIANE ACKERMAN

114

Plead guilty and often to
loving your family and friends.

–DAN ZADRA

Remember that what is hard
to endure will be sweet to recall.

–TOTE YAMADA

It is good to have an end to
journey towards—but it is the journey
that matters, in the end.

–URSULA K. LEGUIN

Keep a diary of your daily wins
and accomplishments. If your life is
worth living, it's worth recording.

–MARILYN GREY

None of us can go it alone.
Support your team.

–DR. ROBERT SCHULLER

116

Learn from the mistakes of others.
You can't possibly live long enough
to make them all yourself.

–SAM LEVENSON

Be assured that most of
your problems will disappear by
themselves if you don't get too
attached to them.

—EDGE KEYNOTE

What appears to be the end of the road
may simply be a bend in the road.

—DR. ROBERT SCHULLER

If your horse dies, get off.

—OLD BUSINESS AXIOM

There will be ebbs and flows.
Remember that the tide always
always comes back.

—UNKNOWN

118

Always know in your heart that
you are far bigger than anything
that can happen to you.

—DAN ZADRA

If you're already walking on
thin ice, why not dance?

—GIL ATKINSON

Don't forget until it's too late
that the business of life is not
about business, but living.

–B. C. FORBES

Many of the things you can count,
don't count. Many of the things you
can't count, really count.

–ALBERT EINSTEIN

Love people. Use things.
Not vice-versa.

–KELLY ANN ROTHAUS

119

When you grow old or ill,
the most important things
to you will be who and
what you've loved.

—JUNE MARTIN

Never think you've
seen the last of anything.

—EUDORA WELTY

As you get older,
don't slow down, speed up.
There's less time left.

—MALCOLM FORBES

120

When the grass appears greener
on the other side of the fence…
fertilize your grass.

–EDGE KEYNOTE

Never let yesterday
use up too much of today.

–KOBI YAMADA

There are only so many tomorrows.

–MICHAEL LANDON

Be gentle and patient
with people. Everyone's bruised.

–KATIE LAMBERT

If you want love, give it away.
If you want friends, be one.
That's how it works.

–DAN ZADRA

Hold a true friend with
both your hands.

–AFRICAN PROVERB

Live each and every day
as if it were your last—because
one day you'll be right.

–BOB MOAWAD

You have not lived a perfect
day unless you've done something
for someone who will never be
able to repay you.

–RUTH SMELTZER

You never know when
you're making a memory.

–RICKIE LEE JONES

123

There's more to life
than having everything.

–MAURICE SENDAK

Be good to yourself.
If you don't take care of your body,
where will you live?

–KOBI YAMADA

For all that has been, Thanks.
For all that will be, Yes.

–DAG HAMMARSKJÖLD

124

Savor life's tiny delights—
a crackling fire, a glorious sunset,
a hug from a child, a walk with a
friend, a kiss behind the ear.

–JOHN ANTHONY

If you don't have all the
things you want, be grateful for
all the things you don't have
that you didn't want.

–GIL ATKINSON

He who laughs, lasts.

–MARY PETTIBONE POOLE

May you live all the days of your life.

—JONATHAN SWIFT